wander the stars

A JOURNAL FOR FINDING INSIGHT THROUGH ASTROLOGY

nina kahn

CASTLE POINT BOOKS
NEW YORK

you're a star baby at heart,

looking deep into space for answers to some of life's greatest mysteries. Or, hey, maybe you're just trying to make more sense of your daily horoscope. Either way, this journal is designed to help you find those answers, one reflective and magical moment at a time, and connect with astrology in a personal way every day. Use these pages to explore your birth chart, learn more about the planets, and vibe with the universe. Have fun filling it with your mystical musings, getting astrologically inspired to meet your love, career, and spiritual goals, and developing a deeper connection with the cosmos.

With the signs, planets, and luminaries guiding your way, you're never alone on this quest for self-awareness. Explore the secrets of astrology—and the magic inside yourself— as you work through this journal and wander the stars.

basic astrology
(for not-so-basic babes)

You don't have to be an astrology expert in order to get the max from this journal — in fact, you can be a total astro-newbie and still vibe out and learn a *ton*. Let's introduce a couple of basic astrological concepts: planets and zodiac signs. Flip back to these pages if you need a refresher as you meander through your cosmic journey.

PLANETS

The Sun: will power, creative expression, and your truest self

The Moon: emotions, moods, and memories

Mercury: communicating, timing, and intellect

Venus: romance, beauty, and luxury

Mars: action, passion, and desire

Jupiter: growth, expansion, and knowledge

Saturn: structure, patience, and responsibility

Uranus: unexpected change, awakening, and disruption

Neptune: illusions, dreams, and the supernatural

Pluto: power, transformation, and extremes

TRACKING THE PLANETS

You don't need to be a professional astrologer to track the planets' placement in the sky at the current moment—simply download an astrology app that includes this feature or check reputable astrology sites or social media pages to find out what sign a planet is in at any given time and whether or not it's retrograde.

ZODIAC SIGNS

ARIES

Element: Fire
Symbol: Ram
Keywords: Fearless · Bold · Competitive
Leadership-oriented · Energized
March 21–April 19

TAURUS

Element: Earth
Symbol: Bull
Keywords: Determined · Reliable
Affectionate · Grounded · Sensual
April 20–May 20

GEMINI

Element: Air
Symbol: Twins
Keywords: Talkative · Witty
Adaptable · Quick · Intelligent
May 21–June 20

CANCER

Element: Water
Symbol: Crab
Keywords: Sensitive · Nurturing
Empathetic · Gentle · Protective
June 21–July 22

LEO

Element: Fire
Symbol: Lion
Keywords: Confident · Attention-loving
Generous · Dramatic · Creative
July 23–August 22

VIRGO

Element: Earth
Symbol: Maiden
Keywords: Analytical · Detail-oriented
Helpful · Observant · Precise
August 23–September 22

LIBRA

Element: Air
Symbol: Scales
Keywords: Balanced · Diplomatic
Charming · Artistic · Refined
September 23–October 22

SCORPIO

Element: Water
Symbol: Scorpion
Keywords: Deep · Mysterious · Intense
Magnetic · Secretive
October 23–November 21

SAGITTARIUS

Element: Fire
Symbol: Archer
Keywords: Optimistic · Adventurous
Philosophical · Free-spirited · Lucky
November 22–December 21

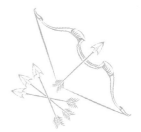

CAPRICORN

Element: Earth
Symbol: Goat
Keywords: Ambitious · Disciplined · Pragmatic
Responsible · Hardworking
December 22–January 19

AQUARIUS

Element: Air
Symbol: Water Bearer
Keywords: Visionary · Unique · Humanitarian
Progressive · Unconventional
January 20–February 18

PISCES

Element: Water
Symbol: Fish
Keywords: Emotional · Dreamy · Mystical
Compassionate · Idealistic
February 19–March 19

my natal chart

Print and paste your natal chart here:

my place in the cosmos

Describe your astrological foundation using your birth chart
to help you. This chart is your origin story. What about
your birth chart do you find most shocking or unexpected?

WHAT PATTERNS, POINTS, PLACEMENTS, OR PLANETARY ASPECTS DO YOU FIND MOST COMPELLING?

WHAT IS A BIRTH CHART?

Think of a birth chart as a snapshot of the universe at the time
of your birth. It's like a fully personalized, one-of-a-kind cosmic
map of *you*, and it can give you tons of insight into who you
are—as well as who you can become. There are plenty of apps
and websites that can generate your personalized natal chart
based purely on your birth date, time, and location. Give it a try!

IN WHICH ZODIAC SIGN DOES EACH OF YOUR NATAL PLANETS RESIDE?

		Zodiac Sign
Sun:	☉	
Moon:	☽	
Mercury:	☿	
Venus:	♀	
Mars:	♂	
Jupiter:	♃	
Saturn:	♄	
Uranus:	⛢	
Neptune:	♆	
Pluto:	♇	

elements of you

It's time to showcase your unique elemental make-up.
Shade in one piece of the pie chart for every zodiac sign you listed
at left. Use the color of that sign's element as it's listed below.

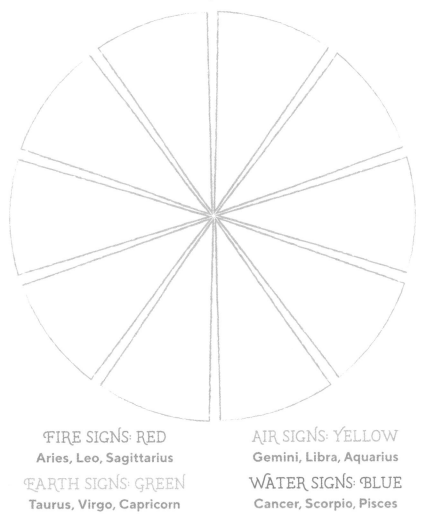

FIRE SIGNS: RED
Aries, Leo, Sagittarius

EARTH SIGNS: GREEN
Taurus, Virgo, Capricorn

AIR SIGNS: YELLOW
Gemini, Libra, Aquarius

WATER SIGNS: BLUE
Cancer, Scorpio, Pisces

WHAT IS THE BALANCE BETWEEN THE ELEMENTS IN YOUR NATAL CHART?

HOW DO YOU RELATE TO YOUR
MOST DOMINANT ELEMENT?

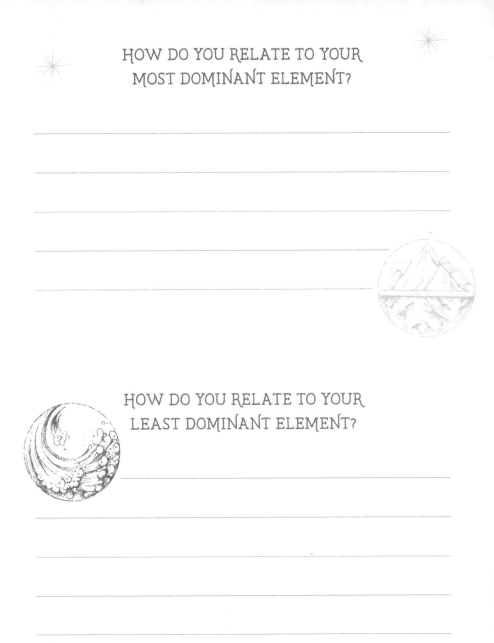

HOW DO YOU RELATE TO YOUR
LEAST DOMINANT ELEMENT?

----

the big three

What's your...

sun sign
(all sides of you; your center)

_____

_____

moon sign
(your private, emotional side)

_____

_____

rising sign or ascendant
(the side you present to the world)

_____

_____

WHAT QUALITIES OF YOUR SUN, MOON, AND RISING SIGNS FEEL MOST AND LEAST ACCURATE TO YOU?

HOW DO YOU SEE YOUR SUN, MOON, AND RISING SIGNS WORKING TOGETHER IN YOUR PERSONALITY?

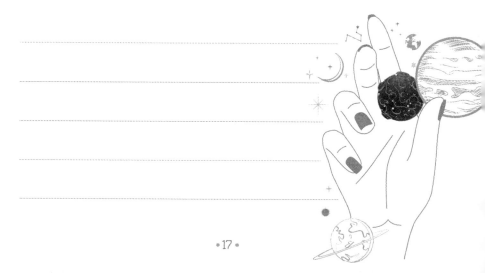

I KNOW NOTHING
WITH ANY CERTAINTY,
but the sight
of the stars
MAKES ME DREAM.

—VINCENT VAN GOGH

HOW ARE YOU ALIGNING WITH THE CURRENT MOON PHASE AND SIGN?

_____

_____

WHAT PLANETS HAVE THE STRONGEST EFFECT ON YOUR LIFE?
HOW HAVE YOU SEEN THIS MANIFEST?

See page 6 for info on each planet's influence.

_____

_____

_____

_____

_____

HOW DO YOU FEEL AND ACT WHEN YOU ARE IN A COMPETITIVE OR DEFENSIVE SITUATION?

(Psst: These are probably your Mars sign qualities!)

WHAT SIDES OF YOU COME OUT WHEN YOU ARE FALLING IN LOVE WITH SOMEONE?

(Psst: These are probably your Venus sign qualities!)

cardinal signs	fixed signs	mutable signs
(Proactive, good at getting things started):	(Steady and persistent, sees things through):	(Prepared for change, flexible and adaptable):
ARIES	TAURUS	GEMINI
CANCER	LEO	VIRGO
LIBRA	SCORPIO	SAGITTARIUS
CAPRICORN	AQUARIUS	PISCES

WHICH OF THESE THREE MODALITIES DO YOU RELATE TO MOST? EXPLAIN WHY.

HOW CAN YOU USE YOUR ZODIAC SIGN'S COSMIC STRENGTH TO EMPOWER YOURSELF AT WORK, IN RELATIONSHIPS, AND BEYOND?

full moon check-in

current moon sign
(circle one):

♈	♉	♊	♋	♌	♍
ARIES	TAURUS	GEMINI	CANCER	LEO	VIRGO

♎	♏	♐	♑	♒	♓
LIBRA	SCORPIO	SAGITTARIUS	CAPRICORN	AQUARIUS	PISCES

Full moons are a time of *illuminations*. This energy vibes best with intentions related to letting go or bringing situations to a climax or conclusion. It's a good time to gather with your astrology-loving friends to celebrate and focus on your relationships with others.

full moon intentions:
What are you letting go of under this full moon?

full moon realizations:
What has been illuminated for you under this full moon?

HOW I'M CELEBRATING
AND HONORING THIS FULL MOON:

love & astrology

spilling the milky way tea

Describe your experiences dating different zodiac signs.
Be honest:

_____

_____

_____

_____

_____

How have you brought astrology into your love life?

_____

_____

_____

_____

_____

horoscope check

DATE

Hop onto your favorite horoscope app or astrology
page and read what it says. What's the vibe?

HOW ARE YOU APPLYING THIS COSMIC ADVICE
AND EMPOWERING YOURSELF
WITH YOUR HOROSCOPE'S ENERGY TODAY?

fire energy

fire signs: aries, leo, sagittarius

passion · action · spirit

What are the most notable planets or points
that you have in the fire signs?

ADD TO THIS LIST OF WAYS
TO CHANNEL FIRE ENERGY

ideas:

do a candle spell · blast your favorite music
say yes to something spontaneous

earth energy

earth signs: taurus, virgo, capricorn

grounded • pragmatic • physical

What are the most notable planets or points
that you have in the earth signs?

ADD TO THIS LIST OF WAYS
TO CHANNEL EARTH ENERGY

ideas:

go on a hike • cook a healthy meal
work with crystal healing

air energy

air signs: gemini, libra, aquarius

social • quick • mental

What are the most notable planets or points
that you have in the air signs?

ADD TO THIS LIST OF WAYS
TO CHANNEL AIR ENERGY

ideas:

watch the clouds • connect with friends
do a visualization meditation

water energy

water signs: cancer, scorpio, pisces

emotional · sensitive · compassionate

What are the most notable planets or points
that you have in the water signs?

ADD TO THIS LIST OF WAYS
TO CHANNEL WATER ENERGY

ideas:

paint with watercolors · visit the beach or a lake
journal about your feelings

THE COSMOS IS
a vast living body,
OF WHICH WE ARE
STILL PARTS.

—D.H. LAWRENCE

TOP SECRET: WHAT'S YOUR LEAST
FAVORITE ZODIAC SIGN, AND WHY?

_____

_____

_____

NOW LOOK AT WHERE YOUR LEAST
FAVORITE SIGN SHOWS UP IN YOUR
BIRTH CHART. WHAT PARTS OF
THAT ENERGY CAN YOU RELATE TO?

_____

_____

_____

_____

DATE

current moon phase
(check one):

☐ ☐ ☐ ☐ ☐ ☐ ☐ ☐

current moon sign
(circle one):

♈	♉	♊	♋	♌	♍
ARIES	TAURUS	GEMINI	CANCER	LEO	VIRGO

♎	♏	♐	♑	♒	♓
LIBRA	SCORPIO	SAGITTARIUS	CAPRICORN	AQUARIUS	PISCES

mood/energy:

struggles:

realizations or areas of growth:

HOW MUCH DOES SOMEONE'S ZODIAC SIGN INFLUENCE YOUR EARLY OPINION OF THEM?

1   2   3   4   5   6   7   8   9   10
(not much)   (ALL of it)

HOW MUCH DOES YOUR DAILY HOROSCOPE AFFECT HOW YOU APPROACH THE DAY?

1   2   3   4   5   6   7   8   9   10
(eh, whatevs)   (it's everything)

HOW MUCH DO YOU RELY ON ASTROLOGY TO DETERMINE YOUR RELATIONSHIP COMPATIBILITY?

1   2   3   4   5   6   7   8   9   10
(barely)   (make or break)

lighting up the luminaries

In astrology, the sun and the moon are known as the luminaries—the two orbs of light that sparkle in the day and nighttime sky. They represent the most well-lit and shadowy sides of your personality, respectively.

WHAT SIDES OF YOURSELF DO YOU SHOW OFF AND PROUDLY BRING INTO THE SPOTLIGHT?

WHAT SHADOWY SIDES EMERGE WHEN YOU'RE ALONE IN THE SAFETY OF THE MOON'S LIGHT?

zodiac doodle

♈	♉	♊	♋	♌	♍
ARIES	TAURUS	GEMINI	CANCER	LEO	VIRGO
♎	♏	♐	♑	♒	♓
LIBRA	SCORPIO	SAGITTARIUS	CAPRICORN	AQUARIUS	PISCES

DOODLE, DRAW, OR MEDITATE ON ANY
OR ALL OF THE ZODIAC SYMBOLS TO CLEAR YOUR
MIND AND LET LOOSE SOME CREATIVITY:

new moon

current moon sign
(circle one):

♈	♉	♊	♋	♌	♍
ARIES	TAURUS	GEMINI	CANCER	LEO	VIRGO

♎	♏	♐	♑	♒	♓
LIBRA	SCORPIO	SAGITTARIUS	CAPRICORN	AQUARIUS	PISCES

New moons are a time of new beginnings. This energy
vibes best with intentions related to starting new things or adding
something new to your life. It's a good time to spend some
quality time alone and get introspective.

new moon intentions:
What are you manifesting under
this new moon?

new moon intuition:
What parts of yourself are you most in
touch with under this new moon?

WHAT ARE SOME IDEAS YOU HAVE
FOR MOON RITUALS?

IF YOU WERE GOING TO START A
WITCHY COVEN FOR MOON RITUALS AND
OTHER COSMIC SPELLS, WHO WOULD
YOU INVITE INTO YOUR CIRCLE?

----

love & astrology

venus power moves

Use this space to generate some date ideas, self-love rituals, or fashion experiments to try based on the energy of your Venus sign.

WHAT ZODIAC SIGNS HAVE YOU
BEEN MOST DRAWN TO THROUGHOUT YOUR
LIFE? WHY DO YOU THINK THAT IS?

_____

_____

_____

WHAT'S YOUR CURRENT FAVORITE
ZODIAC SIGN, AND WHY?

_____

_____

_____

_____

your astrological weekly planner

Each day of the week is aligned with a different planet's energy,
so plan your week to maximize the vibes.

MONDAY
(moon's day)

date:

focus on emotions
& self-care

plan:

TUESDAY
(mars' day)

date:

focus on goals
& action

plan:

WEDNESDAY
(mercury's day)

date:

focus on organization
& logic

plan:

THURSDAY
(jupiter's day)

date:

focus on big-picture
plans & learning

plan:

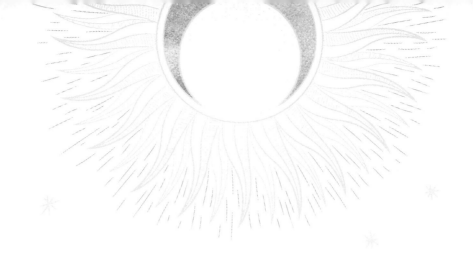

FRIDAY
(venus' day)

date:

focus on beauty,
love & friendship

plan:

SATURDAY
(saturn's day)

date:

focus on
responsibilities

plan:

SUNDAY
(sun's day)

date:

focus on creativity
& self-expression

plan:

DATE

current moon phase
(check one):

☐ ☐ ☐ ☐ ☐ ☐ ☐ ☐

current moon sign
(circle one):

| ♈ | ♉ | ♊ | ♋ | ♌ | ♍ |
| ARIES | TAURUS | GEMINI | CANCER | LEO | VIRGO |

| ♎ | ♏ | ♐ | ♑ | ♒ | ♓ |
| LIBRA | SCORPIO | SAGITTARIUS | CAPRICORN | AQUARIUS | PISCES |

mood/energy:

struggles:

realizations or areas of growth:

HOW DO YOU INCORPORATE ASTROLOGY
INTO YOUR DAILY LIFE?

QUALITIES OF YOUR SIGN THAT YOU
ASPIRE TO EMBRACE MORE DEEPLY:

eclipse check

Eclipse seasons take place about twice a year. Eclipses can happen on a new or full moon, but they almost always bring revelations and dramatic changes. Try meditating or writing down your thoughts below to stay grounded through the shifts.

DATE OF ECLIPSE: _____   ZODIAC SIGN: _____

lunar eclipse / solar eclipse
(circle one)

_____

_____

_____

_____

RETHINK YOUR RITUALS

During an eclipse, you don't want to manifest or perform rituals like you might on a typical full or new moon, as the energy is chaotic and can bring about fateful shifts and unexpected results.

WRITE DOWN ANY ECLIPSE REVELATIONS AND BREAKTHROUGHS YOU HAVE:

REFLECT ON YOUR OVERALL ECLIPSE EXPERIENCE:

love & astrology

your cosmic romance

Identify the house where Venus lives in your birth chart for more insight into your love profile. For example, Venus in the 7th house bodes well for committed relationships. Reflect on your love style, ideal partnership, and romantic tendencies through the lens of your birth chart. Record your musings and discoveries below.

AT HOME IN THE STARS

Houses are what make up your birth chart in astrology and they represent different aspects of your life. There are twelve houses, and each is uniquely ruled by a different sign in your chart. Knowing which house each of your planets reside in on your natal chart can help you learn how that planet's qualities manifest in your life.

THREE THINGS

CANNOT BE LONG HIDDEN:

the sun, the moon and the truth.

—BUDDHA

aries vibes

The cardinal fire sign.

fearless · bold · leadership-oriented · competitive · energized

PLANETS, POINTS, OR HOUSES IN THE SIGN OF ARIES (CHECK YOUR BIRTH CHART!)

ANSWER THESE CELESTIAL REFLECTION QUESTIONS ON ANY DAY WHEN THERE'S HEAVY ARIES ENERGY OR MAJOR MARS-RELATED ASPECTS IN THE SKIES:

In what ways are fears holding you back
from doing what you want?

What are your strongest leadership skills?

What gives you motivation and
willpower to slay your goals?

taurus vibes

The fixed earth sign.

determined · reliable · affectionate · grounded · sensual

PLANETS, POINTS, OR HOUSES IN THE SIGN OF TAURUS (CHECK YOUR BIRTH CHART!)

ANSWER THESE CELESTIAL REFLECTION
QUESTIONS ON ANY DAY WHEN THERE'S
HEAVY TAURUS ENERGY OR MAJOR
VENUS-RELATED ASPECTS IN THE SKIES:

How can you indulge more in simple pleasures
and tune into your physical senses?

_____

_____

What material possessions are most valuable
and important to you, and why?

_____

_____

What do you value most about yourself?

_____

_____

gemini vibes

The mutable air sign.

talkative · witty · adaptable · quick · intelligent

PLANETS, POINTS, OR HOUSES IN THE SIGN OF GEMINI (CHECK YOUR BIRTH CHART!)

ANSWER THESE CELESTIAL REFLECTION QUESTIONS ON ANY DAY WHEN THERE'S HEAVY GEMINI ENERGY OR MAJOR MERCURY-RELATED ASPECTS IN THE SKIES:

What topics, people, and experiences make your mind most active and interested?

How can you bring more curiosity and interest into your life?

How can you be more present with the people, places, and things in your immediate surroundings?

----

cancer vibes

The cardinal water sign.

sensitive · nurturing · empathetic · gentle · protective

PLANETS, POINTS, OR HOUSES IN THE SIGN OF CANCER (CHECK YOUR BIRTH CHART!)

ANSWER THESE CELESTIAL REFLECTION
QUESTIONS ON ANY DAY WHEN THERE'S
HEAVY CANCER ENERGY OR MAJOR
MOON-RELATED ASPECTS IN THE SKIES:

How can you be more in touch with your
feelings and emotions?

_____

_____

What makes you feel most nurtured,
cared for, and comforted?

_____

_____

How can you create more emotional connections
in the world? How can you practice
feeling deeper empathy for other people?

_____

leo vibes

The fixed fire sign.

confident · attention-loving · generous · dramatic · creative

PLANETS, POINTS, OR HOUSES IN THE SIGN OF LEO (CHECK YOUR BIRTH CHART!)

ANSWER THESE CELESTIAL REFLECTION
QUESTIONS ON ANY DAY WHEN THERE'S
HEAVY LEO ENERGY OR MAJOR
SUN-RELATED ASPECTS IN THE SKIES:

What hobbies and activities make you feel
most playful, childlike, and joyful?

What passion projects are you working on
(or would you like to start)?

What are your creative goals? Do they align
with the qualities of your sun sign?

---

virgo vibes

The mutable earth sign.

analytical · detail-oriented · helpful · observant · precise

PLANETS, POINTS, OR HOUSES IN THE SIGN OF VIRGO
(CHECK YOUR BIRTH CHART!)

ANSWER THESE CELESTIAL REFLECTION
QUESTIONS ON ANY DAY WHEN THERE'S
HEAVY VIRGO ENERGY OR MAJOR
MERCURY-RELATED ASPECTS IN THE SKIES:

What areas of your life need to be
reorganized and cleaned up?

_____

_____

What are your current health and wellness goals?

_____

_____

How can you channel Virgo energy to make
the world around you better?

_____

_____

libra vibes

The cardinal air sign.

balanced · diplomatic · charming · artistic · refined

PLANETS, POINTS, OR HOUSES IN THE SIGN OF LIBRA
(CHECK YOUR BIRTH CHART!)

ANSWER THESE CELESTIAL REFLECTION
QUESTIONS ON ANY DAY WHEN THERE'S
HEAVY LIBRA ENERGY OR MAJOR
VENUS-RELATED ASPECTS IN THE SKIES:

What conflicts are you currently facing and how
can you peacefully solve them?

_____

_____

What's the most important thing to you
within partnerships?

_____

_____

How can you bring more balance to your life?

_____

_____

scorpio vibes

The fixed water sign.

deep · mysterious · intense · magnetic · secretive

PLANETS, POINTS, OR HOUSES IN THE SIGN OF SCORPIO (CHECK YOUR BIRTH CHART!)

ANSWER THESE CELESTIAL REFLECTION
QUESTIONS ON ANY DAY WHEN THERE'S
HEAVY SCORPIO ENERGY, OR MAJOR
PLUTO-RELATED ASPECTS IN THE SKIES:

When you think about life's greatest
mysteries, how do you feel?

_____

_____

When have you held back or felt ashamed?
How can you overcome that feeling?

_____

_____

How can you use astrology to deepen intimacy
and trust in yourself and others?

_____

_____

sagittarius vibes

The mutable fire sign.

optimistic · adventurous · philosophical · free-spirited · lucky

PLANETS, POINTS, OR HOUSES IN
THE SIGN OF SAGITTARIUS
(CHECK YOUR BIRTH CHART!)

ANSWER THESE CELESTIAL REFLECTION
QUESTIONS ON ANY DAY WHEN THERE'S
HEAVY SAGITTARIUS ENERGY OR MAJOR
JUPITER-RELATED ASPECTS IN THE SKIES:

If you could travel anywhere in the world right now,
where would you go and why?

_____

_____

Astrology is a liberating force. What about it
makes you feel most free?

_____

_____

How can you bring more optimism
and positivity into your life?

_____

_____

capricorn vibes

The cardinal earth sign.

ambitious · disciplined · pragmatic · responsible · hardworking

PLANETS, POINTS, OR HOUSES IN
THE SIGN OF CAPRICORN
(CHECK YOUR BIRTH CHART!)

ANSWER THESE CELESTIAL REFLECTION
QUESTIONS ON ANY DAY WHEN THERE'S
HEAVY CAPRICORN ENERGY OR MAJOR
SATURN-RELATED ASPECTS IN THE SKIES:

How disciplined are you about
getting things done?

_____

_____

What's your dream job?

_____

What kind of mark do you want to leave
on the world? What legacy?

_____

_____

aquarius vibes

The fixed air sign.

visionary · unique · humanitarian · progressive · unconventional

PLANETS, POINTS, OR HOUSES IN
THE SIGN OF AQUARIUS
(CHECK YOUR BIRTH CHART!)

ANSWER THESE CELESTIAL REFLECTION
QUESTIONS ON ANY DAY WHEN THERE'S
HEAVY AQUARIUS ENERGY OR MAJOR
URANUS-RELATED ASPECTS IN THE SKIES:

What are the things about you that are most unique?

When you think about standing out in a crowd and
being different, what feelings do you have? Why?

What role do you play in your friendship circle or community
at large? What are the joys and struggles of that role?

pisces vibes

The mutable water sign.

emotional · dreamy · mystical · compassionate · idealistic

PLANETS, POINTS, OR HOUSES IN THE SIGN OF PISCES (CHECK YOUR BIRTH CHART!)

ANSWER THESE CELESTIAL REFLECTION
QUESTIONS ON ANY DAY WHEN THERE'S
HEAVY PISCES ENERGY OR MAJOR NEPTUNE-
RELATED ASPECTS IN THE SKIES:

What is your relationship to your dreams?

In what ways do you feel connected to other realms
or the universe on the whole?

How can you connect more deeply to your
own emotions and others' emotions?

THE COSMOS IS
full beyond measure
OF ELEGANT TRUTHS.

—CARL SAGAN

love & astrology
Your Cosmic Romance

WHAT'S YOUR IDEAL ROMANTIC RELATIONSHIP STYLE? DOES IT ALIGN WITH YOUR VENUS SIGN?

HOW CAN YOU USE YOUR VENUS SIGN'S ENERGY TO MEET NEW PEOPLE AND FORM DEEPER RELATIONSHIPS?

your astrological weekly planner

Each day of the week is aligned with a different planets' energy,
so plan your week to maximize on the vibes.

MONDAY
(moon's day)

date:

focus on emotions
& self-care

plan:

TUESDAY
(mars' day)

date:

focus on goals
& action

plan:

WEDNESDAY
(mercury's day)

date:

focus on organization
& logic

plan:

THURSDAY
(jupiter's day)

date:

focus on big-picture
plans & learning

plan:

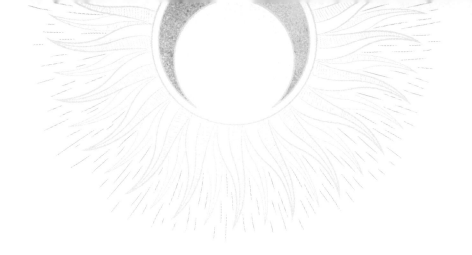

FRIDAY
(venus' day)

date:

focus on beauty,
love & friendship

plan:

SATURDAY
(saturn's day)

date:

focus on
responsibilities

plan:

SUNDAY
(sun's day)

date:

focus on creativity
& self-expression

plan:

mercury retrograde log

These pesky periods happen about three times per year and last for a few weeks. During this time we can experience mishaps and confusion when it comes to communicating, thinking logically, getting around, scheduling events, and managing technology. Track the next retrograde so you can prepare for it and learn from it.

UPCOMING MERCURY RETROGRADE DATES:

BIGGEST FRUSTRATIONS:

BIGGEST TAKEAWAYS:

HOW DOES ASTROLOGY ADD JOY
OR MEANING TO YOUR LIFE?

WHEN AND WHY WERE YOU
FIRST DRAWN TO IT?

HOW IMPORTANT IS SOMEONE'S ZODIAC SIGN WHEN IT COMES TO BEING CLOSE FRIENDS?

1   2   3   4   5   6   7   8   9   10

(who cares?)   (make-or-break info!!!)

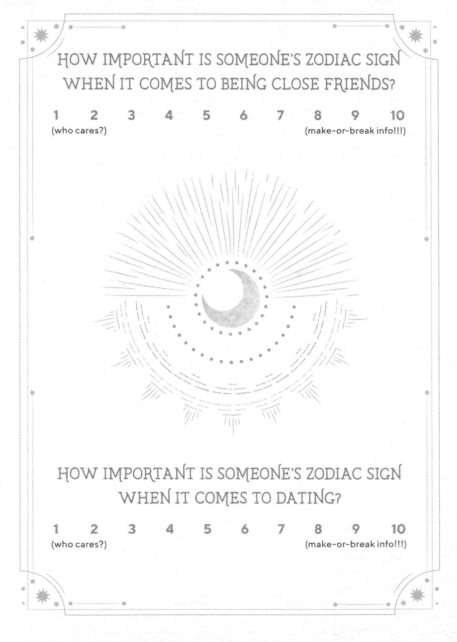

HOW IMPORTANT IS SOMEONE'S ZODIAC SIGN WHEN IT COMES TO DATING?

1   2   3   4   5   6   7   8   9   10

(who cares?)   (make-or-break info!!!)

astrology with a passion

WHAT ARE YOU CURRENTLY FEELING MOST PASSIONATE ABOUT?

HOW CAN YOU FOCUS ON YOUR AMBITIONS AND GOALS GUIDED BY THE ENERGY OF MARS' CURRENT ZODIAC VIBE?

goal crushing
with the moon phases

Set a four-week goal and meet it by aligning it with the energy of the lunar phases. Use this page to track your progress and commit to taking action consistently through the coming moon cycle. Begin during a new moon and focus until the following new moon.

press start

DATE OF NEW MOON:

Write down your current goal and anything you're manifesting.
Write down the steps you're taking to make it happen.

overcome obstacles

DATE OF FIRST QUARTER MOON:

What challenges have you faced over the past week?
Don't give up! What's your plan to overcome them?

celebrate

What have you realized over the past two weeks of working toward
your goals? How are you celebrating your progress?

make space

DATE OF LAST QUARTER MOON:

What are you letting go of as you get closer to your goal?
What new skills or ideas are you making space for in your quest?

cosmic creativity

Let yourself be inspired by the current placement of the sun or moon in the zodiac and make a collage to express your creativity.

LET IT FLOW

Creative expression is especially helpful on days with a lot of water sign sensitivity or fire sign passion!

horoscope check

DATE

Hop onto your favorite horoscope app or astrology
page and read what it says. What's the vibe?

HOW ARE YOU APPLYING THIS COSMIC ADVICE
AND EMPOWERING YOURSELF
WITH YOUR HOROSCOPE'S ENERGY TODAY?

meet your chart ruler

Each zodiac sign is ruled by a planet. The planet that rules your **rising sign** is considered your chart ruler, which means it has a big influence in your life. Circle yours below.

Aries: Mars	**Libra:** Venus
Taurus: Venus	**Scorpio:** Pluto
Gemini: Mercury	**Sagittarius:** Jupiter
Cancer: Moon	**Capricorn:** Saturn
Leo: Sun	**Aquarius:** Uranus
Virgo: Mercury	**Pisces:** Neptune

PLANET ENERGY

the sun
will power, creative expression, and your truest self

the moon
emotions, moods, and memories

mercury
communicating, timing, intellect

venus
romance, beauty, and luxury

mars
action, passion, and desire

jupiter
growth, expansion, and knowledge

saturn
structure, patience, and responsibility

uranus
unexpected change, awakening, and disruption

neptune
illusions, dreams, and the supernatural

pluto
power, transformation, and extremes

DO YOU FEEL CONNECTED TO THE
ENERGY OF YOUR CHART RULER? EXPLAIN.

_____

_____

_____

_____

HOW CAN YOU USE THE ENERGY
OF THIS PLANET/SIGN COMBO TO MAKE
POSITIVE CHANGE IN YOUR LIFE?

_____

_____

_____

_____

new moon

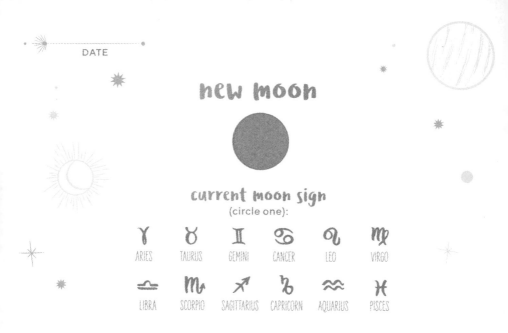

current moon sign
(circle one):

♈	♉	♊	♋	♌	♍
ARIES	TAURUS	GEMINI	CANCER	LEO	VIRGO

♎	♏	♐	♑	♒	♓
LIBRA	SCORPIO	SAGITTARIUS	CAPRICORN	AQUARIUS	PISCES

New moons are a time of new beginnings. This energy vibes best with intentions related to starting new things or adding something new to your life. It's a good time to spend some quality time alone and get introspective.

new moon intentions:
What are you manifesting under this new moon?

new moon intuition:
What parts of yourself are you most in touch with under this new moon?

HOW ARE YOU CELEBRATING AND HONORING THIS NEW MOON?

planetary playlists

What songs capture your zodiac sign's essence, or remind you
of mystical astro-vibes in general? Write out a dreamy zodiac track
list or jot down snippets of your favorite cosmic lyrics.

be humble
FOR YOU ARE
MADE OF EARTH.
be noble
FOR YOU ARE
MADE OF STARS.

—SERBIAN PROVERB

elemental love compatibility

YOUR SUN SIGN:

_____

YOUR PARTNER'S SUN SIGN:

_____

fire signs vibe most with fire & air signs
passion, spontaneity, and lots of excitement

earth signs vibe most with earth & water signs
stability, groundedness, and sensual pleasures

air signs vibe most with air & fire signs
long conversations, mental connections, and social time

water signs vibe most with water & earth signs
creativity, vulnerability, and emotional connection

YOUR SUN SIGN'S ELEMENT

(circle one):

FIRE · EARTH · AIR · WATER

THEIR SUN SIGN'S ELEMENT

(circle one):

FIRE · EARTH · AIR · WATER

HOW DO YOUR SIGNS CONNECT?

_____

_____

_____

HOW DO YOU CLASH?

_____

_____

_____

my crush's zodiac profile

Use your crush or your partner's natal chart to fill
in some of the information below.

moon sign: ....

How do they want to be nurtured?

How do they show they care?

rising sign: ....

What was your first impression of them?

Does their rising sign vibe with their physical appearance?

venus sign: ....

What's their romantic relationship style?

What do they value in love?

mars sign: ....

How do they chase after what they want?

How do they show off their sexy side?

HOW DOES ASTROLOGY ENHANCE
YOUR RELATIONSHIP?

full moon check-in

current moon sign
(circle one):

♈	♉	♊	♋	♌	♍
ARIES	TAURUS	GEMINI	CANCER	LEO	VIRGO

♎	♏	♐	♑	♒	♓
LIBRA	SCORPIO	SAGITTARIUS	CAPRICORN	AQUARIUS	PISCES

Full moons are a time of *illuminations*. This energy vibes best with intentions related to letting go or bringing situations to a climax or conclusion. It's a good time to gather with your astrology-loving friends to celebrate and focus on your relationships with others.

full moon intentions:
What are you letting go of
under this full moon?

full moon realizations:
What has been illuminated for
you under this full moon?

WHAT MAKES YOU FEEL MOST CONNECTED TO NATURE'S CYCLES?

_____

_____

_____

_____

LET'S GET INTERSTELLAR:

What makes you feel most connected to the vastness
of the cosmos and the infinite universe?

_____

_____

_____

_____

cosmic career advice

Look up your *midheaven sign* in your birth chart (it's located at the cusp of your tenth house). This point is all about public recognition, your career, and your legacy. Reflect on the energy of your midheaven sign and how you can manifest it into a cosmically aligned career path or guide you on your current one. Write your thoughts below:

mystical musings

Use this page to make notes about current astrology,
your horoscope, and your recent cosmic findings.

mercury retrograde
before & after

Next Mercury Rx date:

DATE

BEFORE: TIME TO PREP!

**wrap up contracts • have tricky convos
get projects off the ground**

What would you like to finish before the next Mercury retrograde?

_____

_____

_____

_____

_____

_____

_____

AFTER: TIME TO REFLECT!

What have you learned from
experiencing this retrograde?

Did you take the necessary time to slow down,
review, and readjust?

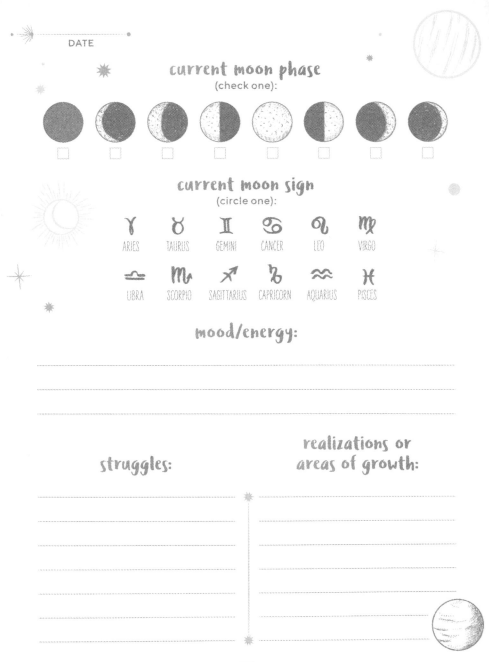

DATE

current moon phase
(check one):

☐ ☐ ☐ ☐ ☐ ☐ ☐ ☐

current moon sign
(circle one):

| ♈ | ♉ | ♊ | ♋ | ♌ | ♍ |
| ARIES | TAURUS | GEMINI | CANCER | LEO | VIRGO |

| ♎ | ♏ | ♐ | ♑ | ♒ | ♓ |
| LIBRA | SCORPIO | SAGITTARIUS | CAPRICORN | AQUARIUS | PISCES |

mood/energy:

struggles:

realizations or areas of growth:

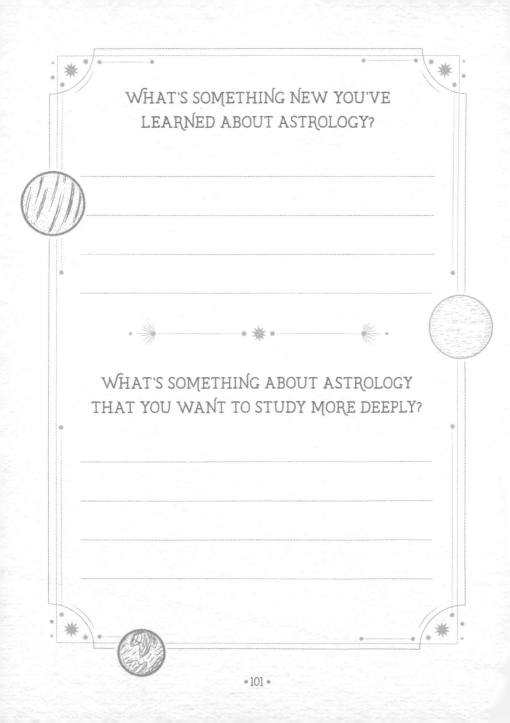

WHAT'S SOMETHING NEW YOU'VE
LEARNED ABOUT ASTROLOGY?

WHAT'S SOMETHING ABOUT ASTROLOGY
THAT YOU WANT TO STUDY MORE DEEPLY?

eclipse check

Eclipse seasons take place about twice a year. Eclipses can happen on a new or full moon, but they almost always bring revelations and dramatic changes. Try meditating or writing down your thoughts below to stay grounded through the shifts.

DATE OF ECLIPSE: ZODIAC SIGN:

lunar eclipse / lunar eclipse
(circle one)

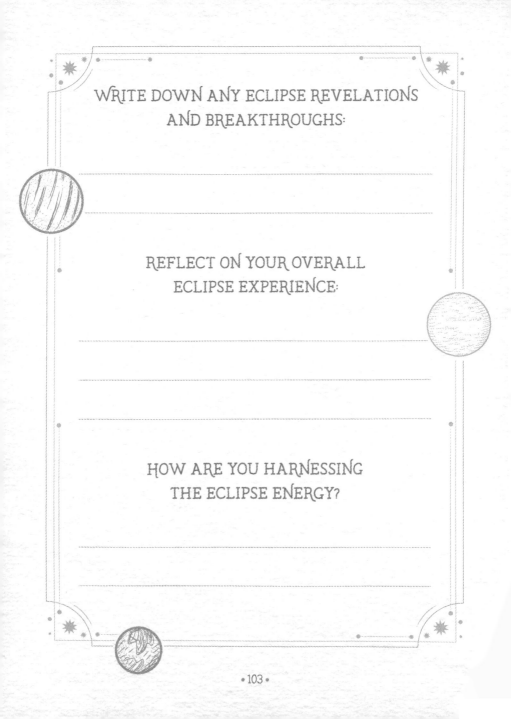

WRITE DOWN ANY ECLIPSE REVELATIONS AND BREAKTHROUGHS:

REFLECT ON YOUR OVERALL ECLIPSE EXPERIENCE:

HOW ARE YOU HARNESSING THE ECLIPSE ENERGY?

inspired by the sun

will power • creative expression • your truest self

your sun sign

the sun's current sign

What do you feel is your driving purpose in life?
How does it align with your sun sign?

_____

_____

HOW ARE YOU USING ASTROLOGY
TO BUILD YOUR CONFIDENCE?

_____

_____

List some ideas for channeling your feelings in a creative way:

_____

_____

inspired by the moon

emotions · moods · memories

your moon sign   **the moon's current sign**

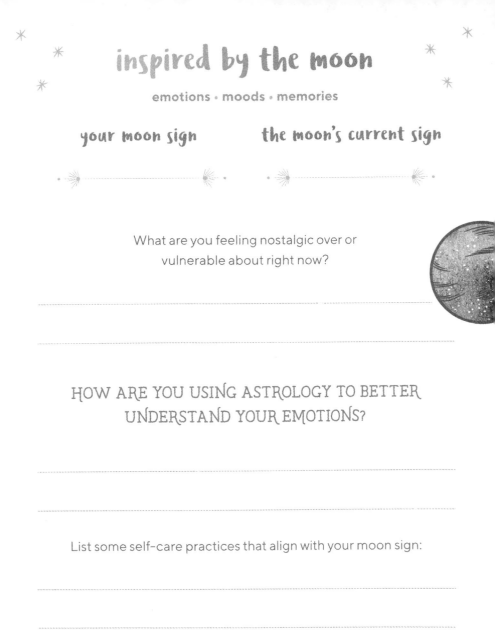

What are you feeling nostalgic over or
vulnerable about right now?

HOW ARE YOU USING ASTROLOGY TO BETTER UNDERSTAND YOUR EMOTIONS?

List some self-care practices that align with your moon sign:

----

inspired by mercury

your mercury sign   mercury's current sign

What's your current preferred style of communication (regular texting, long FaceTime chats, occasionally catching up over coffee, etc.)?

_____

WHAT IS YOUR PREFERRED LEARNING STYLE AS YOU EXPLORE ASTROLOGY AND OTHER MYSTIC ARTS?

_____

_____

List some positive thoughts you can focus on when you're stuck in a negative spiral. Use your Mercury sign's energy for inspiration:

_____

_____

_____

inspired by venus

romance • beauty • luxury

your venus sign

venus' current sign

What are the most sensually pleasurable things you've experienced today? Think visuals, taste, touch, smell, and sound.

LIST THE THINGS THAT MAKE YOU
FEEL MOST LUXURIOUS, LOVED, AND BEAUTIFUL
—AND SMALL WAYS YOU CAN BRING THEM
INTO YOUR EVERYDAY EXPERIENCE.

inspired by mars

action • passion • desire

your mars sign

mars' current sign

What's something you feel competitive about,
and what in your birth chart reflects this?

USING YOUR MARS SIGN AS INSPIRATION,
LIST SOME HEALTHY WAYS YOU CAN RELEASE
YOUR ANGER AND FRUSTRATION:

inspired by jupiter

growth · expansion · knowledge

your jupiter sign
jupiter's current sign

How has learning more about astrology changed your perspective?

IN WHICH SUBJECTS OR AREAS OF YOUR LIFE ARE YOU SEEKING MORE KNOWLEDGE AND EDUCATION?

Write down three positive affirmations to help you focus on success:

1.

2.

3.

inspired by saturn

structure · patience · responsibility

your saturn sign   saturn's current sign

. —≫ ---------------- ≪ .   . —≫ ---------------- ≪ .

What is your relationship with authority?

WHAT TRADITIONS IN YOUR LIFE
HAVE YOU UPHELD OR BROKEN?

List some of the major ways you've
been "adulting" lately:

----

inspired by uranus

your uranus sign

uranus' current sign

Have you had any major awakenings or realizations using astrology?

_____

_____

HOW DO YOU EXPRESS YOUR INNER REBEL?
DOES THIS ALIGN WITH YOUR URANUS SIGN?

_____

_____

List the most unexpected changes that have taken
place in your life lately and how you're adapting to them
(look to your Uranus sign for cosmic advice!):

_____

_____

inspired by neptune

illusions · dreams · the supernatural

your neptune sign   **neptune's current sign**

What have you been daydreaming about lately?

_____

_____

WHAT SPIRITUAL TOOLS AND MYSTICAL PRACTICES ARE YOU MOST DRAWN TO?

_____

_____

List some of your go-to ways for escaping
reality and embracing fantasy:

_____

_____

inspired by pluto

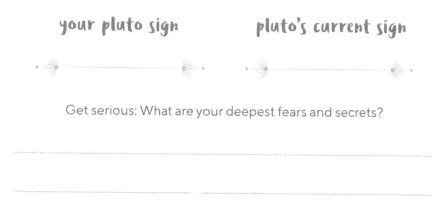

your pluto sign   pluto's current sign

Get serious: What are your deepest fears and secrets?

_____

_____

HOW CAN YOU PULL THESE SECRETS INTO THE
LIGHT AND HEAL THEM. EITHER USING
ASTROLOGY OR THE ENERGY OF YOUR PLUTO SIGN?

_____

_____

List the ways you feel most aligned with your generation:

_____

_____

your astrological weekly planner

Each day of the week is aligned with a different planets' energy,
so plan your week to maximize on the vibes.

MONDAY
(moon's day)

date:

focus on emotions
& self-care

plan:

TUESDAY
(mars' day)

date:

focus on goals
& action

plan:

WEDNESDAY
(mercury's day)

date:

focus on organization
& logic

plan:

THURSDAY
(jupiter's day)

date:

focus on big-picture
plans & learning

plan:

FRIDAY
(venus' day)

date:

focus on beauty,
love & friendship

plan:

SATURDAY
(saturn's day)

date:

focus on
responsibilities

plan:

SUNDAY
(sun's day)

date:

focus on creativity
& self-expression

plan:

planetary doodle

⊙
SUN

☿
MERCURY

♀
VENUS

☽
MOON

♂
MARS

♃
JUPITER

♄
SATURN

⛢
URANUS

♆
NEPTUNE

♇
PLUTO

DOODLE. DRAW. OR MEDITATE ON ANY
OR ALL OF THE PLANETS' SYMBOLS TO CLEAR YOUR
MIND AND CHANNEL SOME CREATIVITY:

IN ALL CHAOS
there is a cosmos,
IN ALL DISORDER
a secret order.

—CARL JUNG

horoscope check

DATE

Hop onto your favorite horoscope app or astrology
page and read what it says. What's the vibe?

HOW ARE YOU APPLYING THIS COSMIC ADVICE
AND EMPOWERING YOURSELF
WITH YOUR HOROSCOPE'S ENERGY TODAY?

Spend some time in the quiet of the night and let
your thoughts wander among the stars. Then come back
to this journal. How do you feel? What visions, feelings,
or questions came into your mind?

_____

_____

_____

WHEN DID YOU FIRST CONTEMPLATE
THE VASTNESS OF THE UNIVERSE?

_____

_____

_____

_____

_____

mercury retrograde log

These pesky periods happen about three times per year and last for a few weeks. During this time we can experience mishaps and confusion when it comes to communicating, thinking logically, getting around, scheduling events, and managing technology. Track the next retrograde so you can prepare for it and learn from it.

UPCOMING MERCURY RETROGRADE DATES:

BIGGEST FRUSTRATIONS:

BIGGEST TAKEAWAYS:

the signs in your life

Everyone you know, organized by zodiac signs:

aries

libra

taurus

scorpio

gemini

sagittarius

cancer

capricorn

leo

aquarius

virgo

pisces

Don't forget to wish them a happy sun sign season!

cosmic dreams

You might have more vivid, intense, or meaningful dreams
when there are powerful Neptune aspects or a full moon.
Write your dreams after waking the night before or after
a full moon or a big Neptunian moment.

DATE

moon placement   **neptune placement**

love & astrology

cosmic crushing

Where is Venus in your crush or partner's birth chart? Use the space below to plan some cute date ideas, swoon-worthy surprises, and romantic playlist tracks for them based on their Venus sign's vibe.

goal crushing
with the moon phases

You know the drill, cosmic cutie: Set a four-week goal and align it with the energy of the lunar phases. Use this page to track your progress and commit to taking action consistently through the coming moon cycle. Begin during a new moon and focus until the following new moon.

press start

DATE OF NEW MOON:

Write down your current goal and anything you're manifesting. Write down the steps you're taking to make it happen.

overcome obstacles

DATE OF FIRST QUARTER MOON:

What challenges have you faced over the past week? Don't give up! What's your plan to overcome them?

celebrate

DATE OF FULL MOON:

What have you realized over the past two weeks of working toward your goals? How are you celebrating your progress?

make space

DATE OF LAST QUARTER MOON:

What are you letting go of as you get closer to your goal? What new skills or ideas are you making space for in your quest?

mystical musings

Use this page to make notes about current astrology,
your horoscope, and your recent cosmic findings.

my astrology readings

The next time you get a professional astrology reading, write about your experience here so you don't forget the deets:

DATE _____

juicy details: _____

_____

_____

DATE _____

juicy details: _____

_____

_____

DATE _____

juicy details: _____

_____

_____

starbaby forever

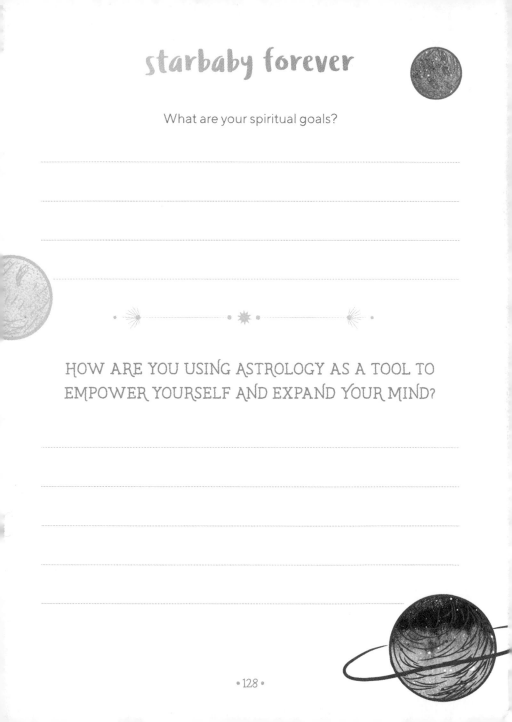

What are your spiritual goals?

HOW ARE YOU USING ASTROLOGY AS A TOOL TO EMPOWER YOURSELF AND EXPAND YOUR MIND?